July

○ 29. MONDAY

○ 30. TUESDAY

○ 31. WEDNESDAY

○ 1. THURSDAY

○ 2. FRIDAY

○ 3. SATURDAY / 4. SUNDAY

August

○ 5. MONDAY

○ 6. TUESDAY

○ 7. WEDNESDAY

○ 8. THURSDAY

○ 9. FRIDAY

○ 10. SATURDAY / 11. SUNDAY

August

○ 12. MONDAY

○ 13. TUESDAY

○ 14. WEDNESDAY

○ 15. THURSDAY

○ 16. FRIDAY

○ 17. SATURDAY / 18. SUNDAY

August

08/19/19 to 08/25/19

○ 19. MONDAY

○ 20. TUESDAY

○ 21. WEDNESDAY

○ 22. THURSDAY

○ 23. FRIDAY

○ 24. SATURDAY / 25. SUNDAY

August

08/26/19 to 09/01/19

○ 26. MONDAY

○ 27. TUESDAY

○ 28. WEDNESDAY

○ 29. THURSDAY

○ 30. FRIDAY

○ 31. SATURDAY / 1. SUNDAY

September

09/02/19 to 09/08/19

○ 2. MONDAY

○ 3. TUESDAY

○ 4. WEDNESDAY

○ 5. THURSDAY

○ 6. FRIDAY

○ 7. SATURDAY / 8. SUNDAY

September

09/09/19 to 09/15/19

○ 9. MONDAY

○ 10. TUESDAY

○ 11. WEDNESDAY

○ 12. THURSDAY

○ 13. FRIDAY

○ 14. SATURDAY / 15. SUNDAY

September

○ 16. MONDAY

○ 17. TUESDAY

○ 18. WEDNESDAY

○ 19. THURSDAY

○ 20. FRIDAY

○ 21. SATURDAY / 22. SUNDAY

September

○ 23. MONDAY

○ 24. TUESDAY

○ 25. WEDNESDAY

○ 26. THURSDAY

○ 27. FRIDAY

○ 28. SATURDAY / 29. SUNDAY

September

○ 30. MONDAY

○ 1. TUESDAY

○ 2. WEDNESDAY

○ 3. THURSDAY

○ 4. FRIDAY

○ 5. SATURDAY / 6. SUNDAY

October

○ 7. MONDAY

○ 8. TUESDAY

○ 9. WEDNESDAY

○ 10. THURSDAY

○ 11. FRIDAY

○ 12. SATURDAY / 13. SUNDAY

October

○ 14. MONDAY

○ 15. TUESDAY

○ 16. WEDNESDAY

○ 17. THURSDAY

○ 18. FRIDAY

○ 19. SATURDAY / 20. SUNDAY

October

○ 21. MONDAY

○ 22. TUESDAY

○ 23. WEDNESDAY

○ 24. THURSDAY

○ 25. FRIDAY

○ 26. SATURDAY / 27. SUNDAY

October

○ 28. MONDAY

○ 29. TUESDAY

○ 30. WEDNESDAY

○ 31. THURSDAY

○ 1. FRIDAY

○ 2. SATURDAY / 3. SUNDAY

November

11/04/19 to 11/10/19

○ 4. MONDAY

○ 5. TUESDAY

○ 6. WEDNESDAY

○ 7. THURSDAY

○ 8. FRIDAY

○ 9. SATURDAY / 10. SUNDAY

November

Week 46   11/11/19 to 11/17/19

○ 11. MONDAY

○ 12. TUESDAY

○ 13. WEDNESDAY

○ 14. THURSDAY

○ 15. FRIDAY

○ 16. SATURDAY / 17. SUNDAY

November

○ 18. MONDAY

○ 19. TUESDAY

○ 20. WEDNESDAY

○ 21. THURSDAY

○ 22. FRIDAY

○ 23. SATURDAY / 24. SUNDAY

November

○ 25. MONDAY

○ 26. TUESDAY

○ 27. WEDNESDAY

○ 28. THURSDAY

○ 29. FRIDAY

○ 30. SATURDAY / 1. SUNDAY

December

12/02/19 to 12/08/19

○ 2. MONDAY

○ 3. TUESDAY

○ 4. WEDNESDAY

○ 5. THURSDAY

○ 6. FRIDAY

○ 7. SATURDAY / 8. SUNDAY

December

12/09/19 to 12/15/19

○ 9. MONDAY

○ 10. TUESDAY

○ 11. WEDNESDAY

○ 12. THURSDAY

○ 13. FRIDAY

○ 14. SATURDAY / 15. SUNDAY

December

12/16/19 to 12/22/19

○ 16. MONDAY

○ 17. TUESDAY

○ 18. WEDNESDAY

○ 19. THURSDAY

○ 20. FRIDAY

○ 21. SATURDAY / 22. SUNDAY

December

○ 23. MONDAY

○ 24. TUESDAY

○ 25. WEDNESDAY

○ 26. THURSDAY

○ 27. FRIDAY

○ 28. SATURDAY / 29. SUNDAY

December

○ 30. MONDAY

○ 31. TUESDAY

○ 1. WEDNESDAY

○ 2. THURSDAY

○ 3. FRIDAY

○ 4. SATURDAY / 5. SUNDAY

January

01/06/20 to 01/12/20

○ 6. MONDAY

○ 7. TUESDAY

○ 8. WEDNESDAY

○ 9. THURSDAY

○ 10. FRIDAY

○ 11. SATURDAY / 12. SUNDAY

January

○ 13. MONDAY

○ 14. TUESDAY

○ 15. WEDNESDAY

○ 16. THURSDAY

○ 17. FRIDAY

○ 18. SATURDAY / 19. SUNDAY

January

○ 20. MONDAY

○ 21. TUESDAY

○ 22. WEDNESDAY

○ 23. THURSDAY

○ 24. FRIDAY

○ 25. SATURDAY / 26. SUNDAY

January

○ 27. MONDAY

○ 28. TUESDAY

○ 29. WEDNESDAY

○ 30. THURSDAY

○ 31. FRIDAY

○ 1. SATURDAY / 2. SUNDAY

February

Week 6   02/03/20 to 02/09/20

○ 3. MONDAY

○ 4. TUESDAY

○ 5. WEDNESDAY

○ 6. THURSDAY

○ 7. FRIDAY

○ 8. SATURDAY / 9. SUNDAY

February

○ 10. MONDAY

○ 11. TUESDAY

○ 12. WEDNESDAY

○ 13. THURSDAY

○ 14. FRIDAY

○ 15. SATURDAY / 16. SUNDAY

February

○ 17. MONDAY

○ 18. TUESDAY

○ 19. WEDNESDAY

○ 20. THURSDAY

○ 21. FRIDAY

○ 22. SATURDAY / 23. SUNDAY

February

○ 24. MONDAY

○ 25. TUESDAY

○ 26. WEDNESDAY

○ 27. THURSDAY

○ 28. FRIDAY

○ 29. SATURDAY / 1. SUNDAY

March

○ 2. MONDAY

○ 3. TUESDAY

○ 4. WEDNESDAY

○ 5. THURSDAY

○ 6. FRIDAY

○ 7. SATURDAY / 8. SUNDAY

March

○ 9. MONDAY

○ 10. TUESDAY

○ 11. WEDNESDAY

○ 12. THURSDAY

○ 13. FRIDAY

○ 14. SATURDAY / 15. SUNDAY

March

○ 16. MONDAY

○ 17. TUESDAY

○ 18. WEDNESDAY

○ 19. THURSDAY

○ 20. FRIDAY

○ 21. SATURDAY / 22. SUNDAY

March

○ 23. MONDAY

○ 24. TUESDAY

○ 25. WEDNESDAY

○ 26. THURSDAY

○ 27. FRIDAY

○ 28. SATURDAY / 29. SUNDAY

March

○ 30. MONDAY

○ 31. TUESDAY

○ 1. WEDNESDAY

○ 2. THURSDAY

○ 3. FRIDAY

○ 4. SATURDAY / 5. SUNDAY

April

○ 6. MONDAY

○ 7. TUESDAY

○ 8. WEDNESDAY

○ 9. THURSDAY

○ 10. FRIDAY

○ 11. SATURDAY / 12. SUNDAY

April

○ 13. MONDAY

○ 14. TUESDAY

○ 15. WEDNESDAY

○ 16. THURSDAY

○ 17. FRIDAY

○ 18. SATURDAY / 19. SUNDAY

April

○ 20. MONDAY

○ 21. TUESDAY

○ 22. WEDNESDAY

○ 23. THURSDAY

○ 24. FRIDAY

○ 25. SATURDAY / 26. SUNDAY

April

04/27/20 to 05/03/20

○ 27. MONDAY

○ 28. TUESDAY

○ 29. WEDNESDAY

○ 30. THURSDAY

○ 1. FRIDAY

○ 2. SATURDAY / 3. SUNDAY

May

○ 4. MONDAY

○ 5. TUESDAY

○ 6. WEDNESDAY

○ 7. THURSDAY

○ 8. FRIDAY

○ 9. SATURDAY / 10. SUNDAY

May

Week 20   05/11/20 to 05/17/20

○ 11. MONDAY

○ 12. TUESDAY

○ 13. WEDNESDAY

○ 14. THURSDAY

○ 15. FRIDAY

○ 16. SATURDAY / 17. SUNDAY

May

○ 18. MONDAY

○ 19. TUESDAY

○ 20. WEDNESDAY

○ 21. THURSDAY

○ 22. FRIDAY

○ 23. SATURDAY / 24. SUNDAY

May

○ 25. MONDAY

○ 26. TUESDAY

○ 27. WEDNESDAY

○ 28. THURSDAY

○ 29. FRIDAY

○ 30. SATURDAY / 31. SUNDAY

June

06/01/20 to 06/07/20

○ 1. MONDAY

○ 2. TUESDAY

○ 3. WEDNESDAY

○ 4. THURSDAY

○ 5. FRIDAY

○ 6. SATURDAY / 7. SUNDAY

June

○ 8. MONDAY

○ 9. TUESDAY

○ 10. WEDNESDAY

○ 11. THURSDAY

○ 12. FRIDAY

○ 13. SATURDAY / 14. SUNDAY

June

Week 25   06/15/20 to 06/21/20

○ 15. MONDAY

○ 16. TUESDAY

○ 17. WEDNESDAY

○ 18. THURSDAY

○ 19. FRIDAY

○ 20. SATURDAY / 21. SUNDAY

June

○ 22. MONDAY

○ 23. TUESDAY

○ 24. WEDNESDAY

○ 25. THURSDAY

○ 26. FRIDAY

○ 27. SATURDAY / 28. SUNDAY

June

○ 29. MONDAY

○ 30. TUESDAY

○ 1. WEDNESDAY

○ 2. THURSDAY

○ 3. FRIDAY

○ 4. SATURDAY / 5. SUNDAY

July

07/06/20 to 07/12/20

○ 6. MONDAY

○ 7. TUESDAY

○ 8. WEDNESDAY

○ 9. THURSDAY

○ 10. FRIDAY

○ 11. SATURDAY / 12. SUNDAY

July

○ 13. MONDAY

○ 14. TUESDAY

○ 15. WEDNESDAY

○ 16. THURSDAY

○ 17. FRIDAY

○ 18. SATURDAY / 19. SUNDAY

July

07/20/20 to 07/26/20

○ 20. MONDAY

○ 21. TUESDAY

○ 22. WEDNESDAY

○ 23. THURSDAY

○ 24. FRIDAY

○ 25. SATURDAY / 26. SUNDAY

July

Week 31   07/27/20 to 08/02/20

○ 27. MONDAY

○ 28. TUESDAY

○ 29. WEDNESDAY

○ 30. THURSDAY

○ 31. FRIDAY

○ 1. SATURDAY / 2. SUNDAY

---

www.ingramcontent.com/pod-product-compliance
Lightning Source LLC
Chambersburg PA
CBHW081019170526

45158CB00010B/3102